The Power of Confidence

7 Ways to Reclaim & Ignite Your Confidence

By CoWano Stanley

Title: The Power of Confidence

Subtitle: 7 Ways to Reclaim & Ignite Your Confidence

Author: CoWano Stanley

ISBN: 979-8-218-44220-0

Table of Contents

Professional Speaker Information

CoWano Stanley is from El Dorado, AR, but she grew up in Minneapolis, MN. She now resides in Las Vegas, NV. At the age of twenty, one of the most remarkable events in her life was the birth of her son. As a single parent, she completed two master's degrees. At the early age of five, she always stated that she would be her boss. So, at the age of twenty-six, she started working in her own cleaning business.

CoWano left the corporate world in accounting in 2018. She became a full-time entrepreneur at 39 years of age. While raising her son, she went through tough times. She began to experience a lack of confidence due to several abusive relationships and challenges as a single parent. CoWano's goals were delayed due to a lack of confidence. She recognized that a change needed to happen. So, she learned how to reclaim & ignite her confidence daily & walk in it boldly. By going through the challenges, she found her passion to help others. So, CoWano started her coaching program & public speaking to teach women the tools on how to reclaim & increase their confidence caused by trauma & life circumstances.

CoWano is the author of five self-published books. She is also a Co-Author in 9 Anthology books, three of them with International Empowerment Speaker Dr. Cheryl Woods and World Leading Motivational Speaker Les Brown. CoWano has been a featured speaker on stage with Dr. Cheryl Woods & Les Brown at You Are Enough & Dare to Rise Above Mediocrity Virtual Conference and SpeakerCon Conference. She has also been a featured speaker on stages of Taurea Vision Avant (New Year New You Conference), JJ Conway (Women Building Wealth Together Conference), Elyshia Brooks (Bigger Bolder You Conference), Dr. Jennifer Harris (I Declare Summit), Angie Renee (Preserve and Inspire Conference) & Grace Quarshie (Women Who Make a Difference Conference in Africa). She has also done a workshop at the 36th Annual Executive Women in Texas Government (EWTG). She was featured in several magazines, such as the Urban CEO Network (2X), Courageous Women, Speakers, Authors All-Star (2X), and Increase Business & Life. She has been seen on US National Times, Making Headline News, Roku, Amazon Fire TV, WWDBTV, Fox News, Small Business Online Network, and interviewed on the Ambitious Women Crowned TV Show.

CoWano will continue to speak and coach women to increase their confidence, due to trauma & life situations, so they can achieve their goals and have unshakeable confidence.

To receive your FREE eBook access to the "Reclaim Your Power in 5 Simple Steps" go to www.myconfidenceiskey.com.

Introduction

Confidence is vital to your self-esteem. It is the belief that you have in yourself that helps direct your path and journey to achieve your goals and endeavors. Confidence is the key to stepping outside of your comfort zone. Confidence is the key to walking into your purpose. Confidence is the key to challenging yourself to be great. So, how serious are you about having unshakeable and unstoppable confidence?

To give you a little back story. My unstoppable and unshakeable confidence came through the experience of three different relationships for a total of sixteen and a half years of domestic violence, physical and verbal abuse, which affected my mental stability. My confidence had diminished and stepped on so much that I did not have any belief in myself. I was a single mother just existing and not living. Over time, the effects caused me to nearly commit suicide. I was around 33 or 34 years of age. By the grace of God, he allowed my son to come into the house that day to check on me. Hearing my son call my name triggered me to think that taking my life was not the answer. I began teaching myself the strategies and tools to reclaim and increase my confidence.

So, this book is to encourage anyone dealing with a lack of confidence that you can do self-work and personal development to acquire the confidence you need to live life and not just exist in life because of life trauma, challenges, and experiences. I pray this book gives you the start to reclaim and ignite your confidence in a way that you can achieve all that you desire. Life will always give unexpected situations, but if you stay tuned into how to respond, you will not fall into a place of counting yourself out.

Chapter 1: Mindset Shift

As you start your journey of reclaiming your confidence, the foundation lies within your mind. It is a mixture of thoughts, beliefs, and perceptions. As a Confidence Coach, speaker, and author, I understand the pivotal role of mindset in shaping your journey. The mindset is more than a lens; it is the GPS of guiding you toward self-discovery and empowerment. It is the change that will move you forward and put you in better places and positions. It will allow you to shift from self-limiting beliefs to unlimited possibilities, from fear to resilience, and from doubt to unwavering self-assurance. When I coach and empower others, one of the main pieces is embracing the new transformation that you can obtain in a resilient and growth-oriented mindset. This chapter will help you understand the essence of mindset. Shifting your mindset will help you breed unshakeable confidence and resilience.

Fixed Mindset vs Growth Mindset

When you understand the difference between fixed and growth mindsets, you can shift your mindset to increase your personal development and confidence. A fixed mindset is rooted in the belief that abilities and intelligence are static traits, limiting progress and resilience. Here is an example of what a fixed mindset person will say: "I'm not naturally talented in this area, so there's no point in trying to improve." Now, let us go right into what the definition of a growth mindset is.

A growth mindset is a belief system that centers on the understanding that abilities, talents, and intelligence can be developed and improved through dedication, effort, and continuous learning. For example, when I started doctoral school, it was challenging because I wasn't used to writing essay papers in a scholarly professional way, but it's a chance for me to learn new skills and improve." So, if you are open to growing personally and professionally to increase your confidence, tapping into a growth mindset is important to adapt to if you do not have that mindset.

Recognizing and Challenging Limiting Beliefs

Confidence starts from the inside and blossoms in the fertile ground of self-awareness, especially when you acknowledge and confront your limiting beliefs. You must start recognizing your internal barriers. What barriers are stopping you? It is a pivotal step toward fostering unshakeable self-assurance.

You need to have a transformative journey by illuminating the hidden confines of self-doubt. You must be able to challenge these beliefs. Sometimes these limiting beliefs start in those whispers of inadequacy or unworthiness. You can get to a place that will anchor in possibility, resilience, and unwavering self-belief. It is up to you to begin nurturing the seeds of confidence, allowing yourself to flourish beyond the confines of your self-imposed limitations. You can get past the limiting beliefs. Some limiting beliefs began when you were taught as a child. Take a moment to think of anything limiting beliefs you grew up with. Challenge yourself to look at things from an unfamiliar perspective.

Adopting a Solution-Oriented Perspective

Confidence flourishes in the fertile soil of a solution-oriented perspective, where challenges become gateways to growth. It is up to you to use the power within to shift your focus from problems to possibilities. It is the action that unlocks a realm of untapped potential, pushing you toward a landscape where creativity, innovation, and confidence intertwine to create a path of infinite growth and success. I encourage you to see obstacles not as roadblocks but as opportunities for innovation and progress. Embracing a solution-oriented mindset does not eliminate the existence of challenges; instead, it amplifies your belief in your capacity to navigate through them. When you adopt this perspective, it turns your setbacks into steppingstones, boosts confidence rooted in the resilience to overcome hurdles, and enables you to thrive in the face of adversity.

Questions to Help with Your Mindset Shift:

What beliefs about yourself have you held for a long time? How have these beliefs influenced your confidence?

_____

_____

_____

_____

Can you identify any limiting beliefs that might be holding you back from achieving your full potential?

_____

_____

_____

_____

Do you tend to view your abilities as fixed or as skills that can be developed? How does this perspective affect your confidence in taking on challenges?

_____

_____

_____

_____

In what areas of your life could adopting a growth mindset significantly impact your confidence?

_____

_____

_____

_____

Notes

Chapter 2: Self-Work

When it comes to "Self-Work," it is a journey that some steer away from. Self-work is necessary for you to reclaim and ignite your confidence, which unfolds complex layers of self-discovery. Self-discovery and the strides of personal growth converge to illuminate the path toward unwavering self-assurance. Self-work should be a part of your daily personal growth. Applying self-work to your daily schedule will increase your confidence. It is a quest toward self-compassion, resilience, and growth. Self-work should be your secret place where you redefine your narratives, shedding the weight of self-doubt and embracing a renewed sense of self-assurance. By doing self-work, you are planting seeds of confidence, nurturing the fertile soil of self-awareness, and moving forward with the unwavering commitment to personal evolution. You are responsible for your journey. No more excuses for why you are not growing within. Let us do the self-work needed.

To receive your FREE eBook access to the "Reclaim Your Power in 5 Simple Steps" go to www.myconfidenceiskey.com.

Reflections

Self-reflection is the mirror that shows you the deepest parts of yourself within. It reveals insight into your thoughts, emotions, and aspirations. It is an intentional pause in the rush of life, a moment where you navigate the pathway of your mind, thinking of your experiences, values, and beliefs. When you are in self-reflection mode, you gain clarity, insight, and understanding. It is the GPS guiding you toward growth and self-awareness. This introspective journey allows us to embrace our strengths, acknowledge our weaknesses, and pave the way for personal evolution. Reflecting on your past, present, and future is a part of being able to ignite and reclaim your confidence. It is within these moments of quiet time that you sow the seeds of self-improvement, resilience, and nurturing the confidence you see in yourself that springs from knowing yourself deeply. So, how often do you take the time to self-reflect on your life?

Accountability

When you want to reclaim and ignite your confidence, self-work is necessary. One part of self-work is self-accountability. It is the core of personal growth. It is a steady commitment to hold yourself responsible for actions, decisions, and consequences. Deciding to take ownership of your behaviors and acknowledging that your choices shape your path is accountability. Through self-accountability, you transform the realm of blame and excuses. You start to embrace a mindset that empowers you rather than restricts you. In developing self-accountability, you become a designer of your progress, build resilience, and strengthen the pillars of your confidence through the integrity of taking ownership of your life.

Discipline

Self-discipline is another part of self-work. It is one that you may have a tough time doing. Self-discipline is a set commitment to staying true to your goals, regardless of obstacles or distractions. Through self-discipline, you can gain the power of consistency, weaving habits that pave the path toward personal growth and achievement. To reclaim and ignite your confidence, you must be able to have self-discipline. Putting it into a daily practice of showing up, pushing boundaries, and embracing discomfort for the sake of progress. Cultivating this virtue lays the foundation for you to have the determination and to nurture the confidence that you desire for your aspirations.

Questions About Self-Work:

What aspects of yourself bring you the most joy or fulfillment?

_____

_____

_____

_____

_____

Are there areas where your actions conflict with your core values? How does this affect your confidence or sense of self?

_____

_____

_____

_____

_____

How do you currently perceive your level of confidence in various areas of your life?

_____

_____

_____

_____

What are your key strengths and areas of expertise that contribute to your confidence?

_____

_____

_____

_____

_____

What situations or events tend to trigger feelings of confidence or self-doubt for you?

_____

_____

_____

_____

_____

Are you accountable to yourself for your actions, goals, and commitments?

_____

_____

_____

_____

_____

What strategies do you use to stay motivated and responsible for your own progress and development?

_____

_____

_____

_____

_____

Do you have external sources of accountability, such as mentors, coaches, or accountability partners?

_____

_____

_____

_____

What habits or practices do you consider essential for maintaining discipline in your life?

_____

_____

_____

_____

_____

What daily habits or routines do you practice to cultivate discipline and reinforce confidence-building behaviors?

_____

_____

_____

_____

_____

Notes

Chapter 3: Embrace Self-Compassion

Do you take the time to nurture kindness and understanding within yourself? Self-compassion is just that. It is about treating yourself with the same care and empathy you offer others. Self-compassion should be a healing power for yourself, mentally and emotionally. It should be the sanctuary where forgiveness meets resilience. Give yourself an invitation and permission to embrace imperfections, release self-judgment, and foster a gentler inner dialogue with yourself. The roadmap to your confidence lies within your self-compassion toward a more profound connection with yourself. It will give you that confidence that blooms. The moment you begin to embrace your self-compassion, it is the root upon which resilience, authenticity, and confidence increase. Start doing the work today of having self-compassion.

Accepting Failure as Opportunities

When taken into effect by self-compassion, accepting failure as an opportunity is part of that. Accepting failure as an opportunity is a journey that challenges people's perceptions of failure. Failure in something does not mean it is the end. It is a crossroad that connects with possibilities. Some people may feel that when they fail at something, they are inadequate or unworthy. This is far from the truth. Failures are steppingstones toward your growth. It is a chance to improve the situation. You can elevate what went right, wrong, etc. You must shift your perspective, viewing setbacks as invaluable lessons. Failure is simply a lesson rather than an indicator of inadequacy. When you fail, get up and try again, and again until you get it right. You build resilience & illustrate the courage to learn from your failures. To ignite confidence, a transformative process of looking at failures as an opportunity is necessary. When you begin to learn from failures, use them to push you closer to completing the goal you started. Failure and quitting should never stop you from getting to the end goal.

Forgiveness and Letting Go

When doing the self-work and self-compassion of the journey to reclaim and ignite your confidence, forgiveness, and letting go will show up. Forgiveness is not about the other person; but it is about you. If you are holding on to something that you need to let go of, it only hinders your progress and blessings longer. When it comes to forgiveness and letting go, some deal with resentment and self-blame. To reclaim your confidence and feel better about yourself, it is time to release the burdens you carry. Instead of holding on to that, God's word says, "Cast your burden on the Lord, and he will sustain you (Psalms 55:22 KJV). Taking the steps to forgiveness & letting go will allow a healing journey toward your self-compassion. It will also allow the scars of your past to transform into pieces of strength. By embracing forgiveness and letting go, you pave the way toward breaking the shackles and chains. Self-doubt leaves, and now you can nurture the fertile soil in which confidence and self-assurance flourish.

Setting Healthy Boundaries

Boundaries are one thing many people fail to set in place when it comes to protecting their confidence and their space. Boundaries should be in your personal and business life. It is vital to reclaim and ignite confidence that unfolds through the art of self-preservation and empowerment. Setting boundaries is a means of asserting your needs, learning to say no without guilt, and nurturing relationships rather than depleting. By having a habit of setting boundaries, you create a path toward keeping healthy relationships, restoring your self-worth, building resilience, and awakening a newfound confidence rooted in self-respect.

Questions About Embracing Self-Compassion:

How do you speak to yourself during tough times or failures? Is your inner dialogue supportive or critical? How does this affect your confidence?

_____

_____

_____

_____

What practices or techniques could you implement to enhance self-compassion and resilience, bolstering your confidence?

_____

_____

_____

_____

What boundaries do you set in your personal and professional life? Are there areas where you feel boundaries are necessary but lacking?

_____

_____

_____

_____

Are there areas where you feel your boundaries are being compromised or where you might need to establish clearer boundaries?

_____

_____

_____

_____

_____

Notes

Chapter 4: Positive Self-Talk

Positive self-talk creates a space for a positive environment. When speaking positively, it improves your mental health and well-being. The more you practice speaking positively, it helps to eliminate the negative thought that comes to mind. What you say out of your mouth matters. God's word says, "Death and life are in the power of the tongue: and they that love it shall the fruit thereof (Proverbs 18:21) KJV)." So, you must be careful of what you say. There are ways to learn how to start speaking positively and consistently. Some of the benefits of speaking positively are reducing depression, reducing anxiety, improving motivation, and better performance. In the subchapter next follows, one of my favorite ways of speaking positively is discussed.

Creating Affirmations

Affirmations are powerful when it comes to speaking positively. Affirmations are simple statements that help to cut out patterns of negative thoughts and beliefs. When used effectively, affirmation can increase your confidence and help you manifest the life you desire. For your affirmation to be powerful, it must be positive, present tense, and precise. You can write your affirmations in a journal and place them on your mirrors and doors. Wherever you can see them consistently. The more you read them, the more you believe them. There will be times when you do not feel the connection to your affirmation. Do not worry, it is just an emotion and a moment you may be going through. Life gives us rainy days and sunny days, but both need to grow. If you have not created your affirmations, then go ahead and start today.

Consistency and Persistence in Affirmation Practice

As I said above, affirmations are powerful if used effectively. To reap the full benefits of affirmations, consistency is key. Affirmations should be a morning routine and meditation sessions for reminders. Make this visible with an affirmation board, journal, affirmation apps, etc. The positive statements at the forefront of your mind will help you to maintain focus and drive throughout your day. Anything you do for 21 days straight will become a habit. So, consistently read your affirmations every day. As your circumstances and mindset evolve, so should your affirmations.

Questions About Positive Self-Talk:

How does the way you talk to yourself influence your confidence levels and decision-making?

_____

_____

_____

_____

When you catch yourself in negative self-talk, what strategies do you use to shift to a more positive perspective?

_____

_____

_____

_____

How does your self-talk influence your ability to pursue and achieve goals? Can you recall a goal you accomplished where positive self-talk played a role?

_____

_____

_____

_____

To receive your FREE eBook access to the "Reclaim Your Power in 5 Simple Steps" go to www.myconfidenceiskey.com.

Notes

_____

_____

_____

_____

_____

_____

_____

_____

_____

_____

_____

_____

_____

_____

_____

_____

Chapter 5: Challenge Yourself

How often do you challenge yourself in areas with which you are not familiar? When it comes to confidence, challenging yourself can boost your confidence. Challenging yourself in new areas may feel uncomfortable and out of place. I understand. Challenging yourself can help you think harder and uniquely. To learn new ways of things, you must challenge yourself. Although challenging yourself can be difficult, it benefits you with personal growth and the discovery of strengths and weaknesses. There are different challenges in life, but below we will talk about three.

Comfort Zone

Can you take a moment, look over your life, and see the times you may have stayed in a comfort zone way too long? The comfort zone is that space where things fit a routine and pattern that minimizes stress and risk. When you are in a comfort zone, you allow yourself to stay stagnant. It is your safe space and mental security. However, the comfort zone keeps you from seeking to enhance your confidence. Stepping out of your comfort zone is vital for personal growth and confidence-building. Each time you step out of your comfort zone, you increase your confidence, gain new experiences, and learn to navigate unfamiliar situations, which builds a wide range of skills and self-assurance. The more you challenge yourself, the more you learn about your capabilities, and the more confident you become.

Facing Fear

If you do not know, fear stands for False Evidence Appearing Real. Fear is a natural and human emotion that can help with personal growth or hindrance. In the context of increasing confidence, learning how to face and manage fear is crucial. By confronting fears, you can break through limits you did not know you had. Fear can be triggered by numerous factors, such as past experiences, trauma, and societal pressures. Facing and overcoming fears will create a reinforcement of a self-image of strength and capability. Remember this scripture that God says, "Fear not, for I am with you; be not dismayed, for I am your God; I will strengthen you, I will help you, I will uphold you with my righteous right hand." Each successful encounter with a fear-inducing situation gives you the power to overcome fear, thereby boosting your confidence. So do not let fear stop you from achieving your goals.

Building Resilience

Now I have bounced back from many setbacks in my life. I know you have too. Resilience is just that. It is the ability to bounce back from setbacks. It is when you can adapt well to change and keep going in the face of adversity. Resilience is a component of confidence. When I lived in my hometown, Minneapolis, Minnesota, and moved to Las Vegas, Nevada, I knew this was a change I needed to adapt to quickly. Now that it has been three years living here, the change is good, and I have adapted well. The change was a struggle. Things were not going as planned or expected. However, I have built resilience by making that change of moving. I not only survived the difficult experience but also used the challenges as opportunities for growth.

Building resilience is essential because it helps you maintain your confidence even when faced with failures, criticisms, or unexpected obstacles. Confidence and resilience are deeply connected. Confidence gives you the belief in your ability to influence outcomes effectively. But resilience provides the tools to recover from setbacks that might break your belief through the process. Together, they create a virtuous cycle: resilience builds confidence by learning to go through challenges and setbacks, and confidence enhances resilience by reinforcing your belief in your abilities.

Questions About Challenging Yourself:

How do you typically respond to challenges or setbacks? Are they seen as opportunities for growth or as roadblocks that diminish your confidence?

_____

_____

_____

_____

_____

Can you recall a time when reframing a challenge positively boosted your confidence? What did you learn from that experience?

_____

_____

_____

_____

_____

_____

How open are you to learning new skills or adapting to change? How does this attitude impact your confidence in navigating different situations?

_____

_____

_____

_____

_____

_____

_____

Notes

Chapter 6: Having a Strong Support System

It is important to have a dedicated support system/circle. This circle can be friends, family, spiritual mentors, business mentors, therapists, etc. Who you surround yourself with matters to your confidence. Throughout life, you need help and sometimes people to talk to. People who will be there to help celebrate the good times and help you through the challenging times. A great support system helps combat mental health issues like depression and anxiety. When creating your support system, make sure it is individuals you trust.

Creating a Supportive Environment

A supportive environment is a foundation that can significantly influence your ability to build and maintain confidence. As a confident coach, I encourage clients to create or seek out environments that affirm and challenge them in healthy ways. Having a healthy and supportive environment nurtures self-assurance but also encourages continuous personal growth. Your environment can be home, work, or in social settings. It affects your self-esteem and confidence levels. Your environment should be positive and provide encouragement, respect, and constructive feedback that helps you feel secure when facing challenges and decisions. Remember, environments that are critical, unsupportive, or dismissive can diminish your confidence and slow personal development.

Questions About Having Strong Support:

Who are the key individuals or influences in your life that affect your confidence positively or negatively?

_____

_____

_____

_____

How could you cultivate a supportive environment that nurtures and enhances your confidence?

_____

_____

_____

_____

What aspects of my environment make me feel safe and supported?

_____

_____

_____

_____

What boundaries do I need to set or reinforce to protect my energy and well-being?

_____

_____

_____

_____

_____

_____

To receive your FREE eBook access to the "Reclaim Your Power in 5 Simple Steps" go to
www.myconfidenceiskey.com.

Notes

Chapter 7: Visualization & Positive Reinforcement

Visualization and positive reinforcement play a key role in reclaiming and igniting your confidence. Visualization is mentally seeing your goals or dreams. Seeing it in your mind before your eyes. When you want something to become reality, you must think about it and see it in your mind first, then stay positive. What you visualize your behavior and action must line up with that. So, it is up to you to discipline yourself with positive reinforcement.

Celebrating Progress and Milestones

One of my favorite parts about increasing confidence is celebration. Celebrating progress and milestones is a powerful practice that can enhance your confidence and motivation. Every accomplishment, small or big, I make sure I celebrate myself. Each accomplishment in my life ignites my confidence. You must acknowledge your achievements, so it reinforces your belief in your abilities and encourages you. Here is why celebrating progress and milestones is essential for confidence:

- Boosts Self-Esteem
- Provides Motivation
- Encourages Growth Mindset

- Builds Momentum
- Reinforces Positive Habits
- Cultivates a Positive Mindset
- Strengthens Resilience
- Inspires Others

Continuous Learning and Improvement

In life, you should grow and mature, not stay the same. Continuous learning and improvement are essential elements of confidence-building. Embracing a mindset of growth and challenging yourself to expand your knowledge and skills can significantly enhance your confidence in various areas of life. Continuous learning and improvement will allow you to have a lifelong journey of commitment to self-development to embark on unshakeable confidence. By embracing a foundation of growth, you open yourself to a world of possibilities, where challenges become opportunities and setbacks become steppingstones toward greater achievement.

Learning is not just about acquiring knowledge but also about experience and learning new skills. Continuous learning and improvement are not just pathways to success; they are the cornerstones of unwavering confidence. You must be willing to unlock your full potential, overcome obstacles, and achieve your goals with confidence and resilience. Remember that a lifelong period of continuous learning and improvement comes with knowledge, discovery, growth, and unlimited confidence.

Questions About Visualization Positive Reinforcement

Have you ever used visualization techniques to imagine achieving your goals? How did this affect your confidence or motivation?

_____

_____

_____

_____

How often do I acknowledge and celebrate my achievements, and how can I do this more regularly?

_____

_____

_____

_____

How do you currently incorporate positive reinforcement into your daily routine?

_____

_____

_____

_____

How do you align your visualization practice with your long-term goals and aspirations?

_____

_____

_____

_____

_____

To receive your FREE eBook access to the "Reclaim Your Power in 5 Simple Steps" go to
www.myconfidenceiskey.com.

Message From the Author

It is understood that life will come with some difficulties. They will be expected and unexpected. However, the unexpected ones are the ones that will throw you into a loop. So, the reaction to those unexpected life situations is what matters. There is a quote that says, "Life is 10% what happens to you and 90% how you react to it." — Charles R. Swindol. I encourage you to always believe in yourself, no matter what reality looks like. Life gives us lessons and tests. But it is up to you to pay attention in those moments. The one thing I know to be true is that things always work out together for your good.

Follow your path and move to the beat of your drums, and everything will be ok. Get on a journey of continuing self-work of your inner self so that the mind, body, and spirit align positively and effectively. Be careful of the company you keep, watch your surroundings, and always set boundaries so that you can be in a healthy space with yourself and other relationships.

I pray this book has encouraged you to have the confidence you need in life that propels you to move forward in the present and into the future that is waiting for you. Now go out there and achieve all your goals and live.

Affirmations to Speak Life

I believe in my abilities and potential.
My value is not determined by others' opinions.
I am proud of my accomplishments, big and small.
I deserve happiness and success.
I am confident in facing challenges in life.
I trust myself to make the right decisions.
I deserve all the good things life has to offer.
I am enough.
I choose peace and calmness.
I release fear and embrace courage and confidence.
I am resilient and capable of bouncing back.
I let go of what does not serve me and embrace what
supports me.
I am the creator of my own happiness, and I choose myself.
I radiate Beauty, Grace, and charm.
I am in charge of how I feel, and today I choose happiness.
I am healthy and wealthy.
I manifest my dreams with ease.
I am surrounded by abundance, and I'm grateful for all that
I have.
I attract positivity and good energy around me.
I love myself.
I am worthy.
I release fear and anxiety.
I love and respect myself.
I will stop worrying about everything.
I will live a healthy lifestyle.
I will forgive myself and others.
I will do what I love.
I will take things on with a gentle approach.
I will stop feeling the need to control everything.

Bible Verses That are Helpful

- Hebrews 10:35; Cast not away therefore your confidence, which hath great recompense of reward.
- Jeremiah 29:1; For I know the plans I have for you," declares the Lord, "plans to prosper you and not to harm you, plans to give you hope and a future.
- John 5:14; And this is the confidence that we have in him, that, if we ask anything according to his will, he heareth us.
- Proverbs 3:26; For the LORD shall be thy confidence and shall keep thy foot from being taken.
- 2 Cor 7:16; I rejoice therefore that I have confidence in you in all things.
- 2 Sam 22:33; God is my strength and power: and he maketh my way perfect.
- 1 Chron 16:11; Seek the LORD and his strength, seek his face continually.
- Proverbs 3: 5-6; Trust in the LORD with all thine heart; and lean not unto thine own understanding. In all thy ways acknowledge him, and he shall direct thy paths.

Social Media Follow

Website: www.cowanostanley.com
IG: startupwomenalliance
IG: loveme_coco
Linkedin: cowanostanley
FB: cowanococostanley
TikTok: cowanostanley
Twitter: cowanostanley
YouTube: cowanococostanley

Request CoWano Stanley to speak at your next Event/Conference

https://form.jotform.com/cstanley326/booking

www.ingramcontent.com/pod-product-compliance
Lightning Source LLC
Chambersburg PA
CBHW060623030426
42337CB00018B/3171
9798218442200